Benjamin Zephaniah

Verses of Resilience, Activism, and Cultural Renaissance

By

Neil Potter

About the author

Neil Potter, the insightful author behind "Benjamin Zephaniah: Verses of Resilience, Activism, and Cultural Renaissance," possesses a deep appreciation for the transformative power of literature and the profound impact of cultural influencers. With a keen eye for capturing the essence of individuals who shape our world, Potter dedicates his craft to unraveling the life and legacy of the remarkable Benjamin Zephaniah.

An avid admirer of poetic expression and social advocacy, Neil Potter brings a unique perspective to the exploration of Zephaniah's journey. Through meticulous research and a passion for storytelling, Potter endeavors to shed light on the intricacies of Zephaniah's life, weaving a narrative that goes beyond the surface, delving into the resilience, activism, and cultural contributions that define the poet's legacy.

Potter's commitment to portraying the multifaceted layers of Zephaniah's experiences is evident in every page of this compelling biography. As an author deeply attuned to the nuances of storytelling, he invites readers to embark on a captivating journey through the life of Benjamin Zephaniah, inviting them to discover the verses of resilience, the echoes of activism, and the vibrant tapestry of cultural renaissance that shape the essence of this remarkable individual.

"Benjamin Zephaniah: Verses of Resilience, Activism, and Cultural Renaissance" stands as a testament to Neil Potter's dedication to capturing the spirit of influential figures and bringing their stories to life for readers eager to explore the intersection of literature, activism, and cultural impact.

Appreciation

Dear Reader,

Thank you for choosing "Benjamin Zephaniah: Verses of Resilience, Activism, and Cultural Renaissance" authored by Neil Potter. Your decision to embark on this literary journey is truly appreciated.

In these pages, you'll discover the captivating life and legacy of Benjamin Zephaniah, explored with depth, nuance, and a passion for storytelling. Neil Potter's commitment to unveiling the verses of resilience, the echoes of activism, and the cultural renaissance within Zephaniah's narrative is evident throughout the book.

As you delve into the pages, may you find inspiration in the remarkable journey of Benjamin Zephaniah, a poet whose life transcends the boundaries of literature, leaving an indelible mark on the realms of activism and cultural transformation.

Your support in acquiring this book not only fosters a connection with the narratives within but also contributes to the celebration of literature, art, and the exploration of influential lives. We hope the insights gained from these pages resonate with you and add value to your reading experience.

Thank you for being a part of this literary journey. Happy reading!

Warm regards,

Neil Potter

Benjamin Zephaniah

Copyright

Copyright © 2023 by Neil Potter

Dedication

To the spirit of resilience, the echoes of activism, and the vibrant tapestry of cultural renaissance that define Benjamin Zephaniah's legacy.

This book is dedicated to those who find inspiration in the verses of life, the rhythm of change, and the transformative power of words. May these pages resonate with the seekers, the dreamers, and the advocates of a more just and enlightened world.

In memory of the indomitable spirit of Benjamin Zephaniah, whose life journey continues to inspire and shape the narratives of resilience, activism, and cultural rebirth.

— Neil Potter —

Benjamin Zephaniah

Table of contents

Benjamin Zephaniah

Benjamin Zephaniah

Impactful works in literature and their societal influence

Chapter Four: Activism and Advocacy

Zephaniah's commitment to social and political causes

Involvement in activism, including anti-racism and human rights

Reflection on his role as a public figure and advocate

Chapter Five: Personal Life

Insights into Zephaniah's personal relationships and family

Balancing public life with private experiences

Chapter Six: Challenges and Triumphs

Benjamin Zephaniah

Summarizing the key aspects of Benjamin Zephaniah's life

Reflecting on the broader significance of his legacy

Achievements

Introduction

The introduction to Benjamin Zephaniah's biography sets the stage for a captivating exploration of the life and contributions of a remarkable individual. Born in Birmingham, Zephaniah emerged as a prominent figure in the UK's artistic and activist landscape. From his early encounters with poetry to his rise to international acclaim, this biography delves into the multifaceted layers of his identity. As we navigate through his artistic achievements, advocacy endeavors, personal challenges, and triumphs, the reader will gain a comprehensive understanding of the man behind the words—Benjamin Zephaniah. This biography seeks to unravel the threads of his life, weaving a narrative that not only celebrates his legacy but also explores the profound impact he has had on literature, activism, and the world at large.

Brief overview of Benjamin Zephaniah's significance

Benjamin Zephaniah stands as a towering figure known for his profound impact on literature, music, and activism. Hailing from Birmingham, he rose to prominence as a pioneering poet, captivating audiences with his powerful words and unique style. Beyond his artistic endeavors, Zephaniah is revered for his unwavering commitment to social justice, tackling issues of racism, human rights, and inequality. His significance lies not only in his creative contributions but also in his role as a formidable advocate, using his platform to challenge societal norms and inspire change.

Setting the stage for his impactful life and career

The stage for Benjamin Zephaniah's impactful life and career is set against the backdrop of Birmingham, where his journey began. Growing up in a city marked by diversity and challenges, Zephaniah's early experiences shaped his unique perspective on the world. As a young artist finding his voice, he navigated through the vibrant cultural scene of the UK, eventually breaking into the poetry realm with a distinctive style that resonated with audiences. Against the backdrop of societal shifts and cultural evolution, Zephaniah's journey unfolds, marked by a passion for creativity and a commitment to addressing pressing social issues. This setting lays the foundation for an exploration of the remarkable life and career that follows.

Chapter One: Early Life

Benjamin Zephaniah's early life is rooted in the vibrant city of Birmingham, where he was born. Growing up in Handsworth, a neighborhood with a rich cultural tapestry, he experienced the diversity and challenges that would later influence his work. Raised in a Jamaican household, Zephaniah's cultural heritage played a pivotal role in shaping his identity and worldview. Early encounters with systemic injustices and a burgeoning interest in poetry became defining elements of his formative years. As he navigated the complexities of adolescence, the seeds of his artistic and activist inclinations were sown, laying the groundwork for the impactful journey that awaited him.

Birth and childhood in Birmingham

Benjamin Zephaniah was born on April 15, 1958, in Birmingham, United Kingdom. His childhood unfolded in the culturally rich and diverse neighborhood of Handsworth. Growing up in post-war Britain, Zephaniah experienced the challenges of racial tension and social change, which would later become central themes in his artistic and activist pursuits. Raised in a Jamaican household, the influence of his Caribbean heritage provided a strong foundation for his identity. Birmingham's dynamic atmosphere, marked by both cultural diversity and socio-economic struggles, served as a backdrop to his early years, influencing his perceptions and sparking the beginning of a remarkable journey that would shape the course of his life.

Influences and early experiences shaping his worldview

Benjamin Zephaniah's worldview was profoundly shaped by a combination of cultural influences and early life experiences. Growing up in a Jamaican household in Handsworth, he was immersed in the traditions, rhythms, and stories of his Caribbean heritage. The rich tapestry of Birmingham's multicultural environment further exposed him to a diversity of perspectives.

Zephaniah's early experiences with racism and social injustice left an indelible mark, fueling a sense of purpose and a commitment to addressing these issues through his art. His encounters with inequality became a driving force, motivating him to use his voice to speak out against systemic challenges.

Additionally, the vibrant atmosphere of the reggae and punk scenes in Birmingham during his formative years played a role in shaping his artistic sensibilities. The fusion of these influences contributed to the development of Zephaniah's unique voice—a voice that would later resonate globally and make a lasting impact on literature and activism.

Initial encounters with poetry and activism

Benjamin Zephaniah's initial encounters with poetry and activism were pivotal moments that laid the foundation for his influential career. As a teenager, he discovered a passion for poetry, using it as a means to articulate his thoughts on social issues and to express his experiences as a young Black man in Britain.

Zephaniah's early activism took root in the local struggles against racism and inequality. Birmingham's charged socio-political climate during the 1970s provided a backdrop for his involvement in grassroots movements and protests. These experiences fueled his determination to address systemic injustices, setting the stage for the fusion of his poetic expression with a commitment to social change.

The convergence of poetry and activism became a defining feature of Zephaniah's work, showcasing his belief in the transformative power of art to challenge and reshape the world around him. These formative encounters marked the beginning of a lifelong journey dedicated to both the written word and the pursuit of justice.

Chapter Two: Rise to Prominence

Benjamin Zephaniah's rise to prominence is a compelling narrative of artistic brilliance and societal impact. His breakthrough in the UK poetry scene during the late 1970s and early 1980s marked the emergence of a distinct voice that resonated with audiences. Zephaniah's performances, characterized by a dynamic fusion of spoken word and reggae rhythms, captivated listeners and set him apart as a trailblazer in the realm of performance poetry.

The release of his first poetry collection, "Pen Rhythm," in 1980, further solidified his standing in literary circles. Zephaniah's ability to seamlessly blend traditional poetic forms with contemporary language and themes garnered widespread acclaim.

As his influence transcended literary boundaries, Zephaniah explored other art forms, including music. Collaborations with renowned musicians added another layer to his creative portfolio, contributing to his recognition on an international scale.

Throughout his rise to prominence, Zephaniah remained unwavering in his commitment to addressing societal issues. His work became a catalyst for important conversations on race, identity, and social justice, firmly establishing him as not only a poetic luminary but also a powerful advocate for change.

Breakthrough in the UK poetry scene

Benjamin Zephaniah's breakthrough in the UK poetry scene marked a transformative moment in the landscape of spoken word and performance poetry. During the late 1970s and early 1980s, he became a pioneering figure, challenging conventional poetic norms with his dynamic and engaging delivery.

Zephaniah's performances, characterized by a potent blend of reggae rhythms and spoken word, resonated with diverse audiences. His ability to weave together socio-political commentary with personal narratives set him apart, attracting attention and admiration from both literary circles and grassroots communities.

The vibrant energy of Zephaniah's live performances, often accompanied by musicians, created a unique and immersive experience for audiences. This innovative approach to poetry not only expanded the reach of his work but also redefined the possibilities of poetic expression in a live setting.

His breakthrough marked a turning point in the perception of poetry as a medium for social commentary, paving the way for a new generation of poets to embrace diverse forms of expression. Zephaniah's impact on the UK poetry scene remains indelible, leaving a lasting legacy that transcends traditional boundaries.

Exploration of various art forms: poetry, music, and writing

Benjamin Zephaniah's exploration of various art forms reflects a multifaceted creative journey that extends beyond traditional boundaries.

- **Poetry:**

Zephaniah's roots lie in poetry, where he initially gained recognition for his dynamic and socially charged performances. His poetry, often infused with rhythmic cadence and vivid imagery, served as a powerful vehicle for expressing personal experiences and addressing societal issues.

- **Music:**

Beyond the written word, Zephaniah ventured into the realm of music, collaborating with musicians to create a unique fusion of reggae, dub, and spoken word. This musical dimension added a dynamic layer to his artistic repertoire, showcasing his versatility and expanding his audience reach.

- **Writing:**

Zephaniah's talent extends to the written word in various forms. He has authored novels, children's books, and plays, showcasing a diverse literary range. His written works delve into themes of identity, race, and social justice, demonstrating a commitment to using literature as a tool for reflection and change.

This exploration across art forms highlights Zephaniah's ability to transcend creative boundaries, allowing his ideas and messages to resonate through different mediums, enriching the cultural landscape with a unique and influential voice.

Key milestones leading to national and international recognition

• **Breakthrough Performances:**

Zephaniah's electrifying performances in the late 1970s and early 1980s, marked by a fusion of reggae and spoken word, garnered attention in the UK poetry scene. These breakthrough live performances laid the groundwork for his national recognition.

• **"Pen Rhythm" (1980):**

The release of Zephaniah's first poetry collection, "Pen Rhythm," marked a key milestone in his literary career. The collection showcased his distinctive voice and thematic depth, earning critical acclaim and contributing to his growing reputation.

- ## **Collaborations with Musicians:**

Zephaniah's collaborations with musicians, particularly in the realm of reggae and dub, expanded his reach beyond literature. These musical endeavors, such as working with renowned artists like The Wailers, played a crucial role in gaining international recognition.

- ## **Television Appearances:**

Zephaniah's appearances on television programs in the 1980s and 1990s exposed him to broader audiences. His magnetic presence and powerful performances on mainstream platforms contributed to his national visibility.

- ## **Honors and Awards:**

Recognition through honors and awards, including being appointed as a Commander of the Order of the British Empire (CBE) in

2008, further elevated Zephaniah's status nationally. Such accolades acknowledged not only his artistic contributions but also his impact on society.

- **Global Impact:**

Zephaniah's advocacy for social justice and his ability to connect with universal themes contributed to his international recognition. His works resonated with audiences worldwide, solidifying his position as a globally influential artist and activist.

These key milestones collectively propelled Benjamin Zephaniah from local acclaim to national and international recognition, establishing him as a leading figure in literature, performance, and activism.

Chapter Three: Artistic Achievements

Benjamin Zephaniah's artistic achievements span a rich and diverse spectrum, reflecting his mastery across various forms of expression:

- **Poetry Collections:**

Zephaniah's poetry collections, including "Pen Rhythm" (1980), "The Dread Affair" (1985), and "Funky Chickens" (1996), showcase his ability to blend traditional poetic forms with contemporary language. His poetry explores themes of identity, love, and social justice with a distinctive rhythmic and lyrical style.

- **Performance Poetry:**

Renowned for his dynamic live performances, Zephaniah pioneered a unique blend of spoken word and reggae rhythms. His captivating stage presence and ability to engage diverse audiences contributed significantly to the evolution of performance poetry.

- **Music Collaborations:**

Venturing into the realm of music, Zephaniah collaborated with iconic musicians, including The Wailers. His contributions to reggae and dub music added a musical dimension to his artistic portfolio, creating a fusion of spoken word and rhythms.

- **Novels and Writing:**

Zephaniah's talents extend to prose with novels like "Face" (1999) and "Gangsta Rap" (2004). His writing delves into themes of social issues, race, and identity, showcasing a versatility that transcends genres.

- ## **Children's Literature:**

Contributing to children's literature, Zephaniah authored works like "We Are Britain!" (2002), introducing young readers to themes of diversity, tolerance, and inclusivity through engaging narratives.

- ## **Playwriting:**

Zephaniah has ventured into playwriting, with works like "Playing the Right Tune" (2008). His exploration of drama further highlights his ability to convey powerful messages through different artistic mediums.

- ## **Advocacy through Art:**

Beyond specific artistic forms, Zephaniah's overarching achievement lies in his use of art as a tool for advocacy. Addressing social issues such as racism and inequality, he has

Benjamin Zephaniah

demonstrated the transformative power of art in fostering dialogue and societal change.

Benjamin Zephaniah's artistic achievements collectively contribute to a legacy that transcends genres, resonating with audiences across literature, poetry, music, and social activism.

Overview of Zephaniah's notable poetry collections

- **"Pen Rhythm" (1980):**

This debut collection marked Benjamin Zephaniah's entry into the literary scene. With a rhythmic and energetic style, it set the tone for his future works, exploring themes of identity, heritage, and societal challenges.

- **"The Dread Affair" (1985):**

This collection further solidified Zephaniah's reputation as a poet of social conscience. Addressing issues of racism and inequality, the poems in "The Dread Affair" showcase a blend of passion and insight.

- ## "City Psalms" (1992):

In this collection, Zephaniah delves into the urban landscape, offering poetic reflections on city life. The poems capture the vibrancy, struggles, and diversity of urban existence, adding a new dimension to his body of work.

- ## "Funky Chickens" (1996):

Known for its humor and social commentary, "Funky Chickens" features a mix of playful and thought-provoking poems. Zephaniah's ability to balance levity with profound insights is evident in this collection.

- ## "Too Black, Too Strong" (2001):

The title itself encapsulates the boldness of Zephaniah's voice in this collection. Exploring themes of racial identity and empowerment, the poems resonate with a powerful call for justice and equality.

- **"Rasta Time in Palestine" (2011):**

This collection reflects Zephaniah's global perspective, addressing political and social issues on an international scale. The poems touch on themes of conflict, justice, and solidarity.

- **"The Life and Rhymes of Benjamin Zephaniah" (2018):**

In this autobiographical collection, Zephaniah weaves together poetry and prose, offering a personal reflection on his life, experiences, and the socio-political landscape. It provides readers with a deeper understanding of the poet behind the verses.

These notable poetry collections collectively showcase the evolution of Benjamin Zephaniah's poetic style and thematic range. From his early exploration of identity to his later global perspectives, each collection

Benjamin Zephaniah

contributes to his legacy as a poet of
profound depth and societal impact.

Exploration of his music career and collaborations

Benjamin Zephaniah's exploration of music and collaborations expanded his artistic reach beyond poetry, showcasing his versatility and influence in the world of sound. Here are key aspects of his music career:

- **Reggae and Dub Fusion:**

Zephaniah seamlessly blended his poetic prowess with reggae and dub rhythms, creating a unique and captivating musical experience. This fusion not only added a distinctive layer to his artistry but also contributed to the reggae music scene.

- **Collaborations with The Wailers:**

One of the noteworthy collaborations in Zephaniah's music career was with the legendary reggae band, The Wailers. This collaboration produced works that bridged the worlds of poetry and reggae, amplifying the impact of his messages through the infectious beats and melodies.

- **"Dub Ranting" (2001):**

Zephaniah released an album titled "Dub Ranting," which exemplifies his exploration of dub music. The album features his spoken word performances set against a backdrop of dub-influenced rhythms, showcasing a seamless integration of poetry and music.

- **Live Performances with Musicians:**

Zephaniah's live performances often included collaborations with musicians, creating an immersive and dynamic experience for audiences. The synergy between his spoken word and live instrumentation elevated the impact of his message.

- **Influence on the Spoken Word Music Genre:**

Zephaniah's contributions played a role in shaping the spoken word music genre. By incorporating socially conscious poetry into musical compositions, he helped pave the way for other artists exploring the intersection of spoken word and music.

Through his music career and collaborations, Benjamin Zephaniah extended the boundaries of artistic expression, using rhythm and melody as vehicles to amplify his messages of social justice and cultural awareness. This musical exploration added a dynamic dimension to his legacy, resonating with audiences across different creative realms.

Benjamin Zephaniah

Impactful works in literature and their societal influence

- **"The Dread Affair" (1985):**

This collection of poems addresses the pervasive issues of racism and inequality, showcasing Zephaniah's ability to use literature as a vehicle for social critique. The poems resonate with a call for justice and equality, leaving a lasting impact on readers' perceptions of societal challenges.

- **"Face" (1999):**

Zephaniah's novel "Face" delves into the experiences of a young man navigating issues of identity and racial tension in a diverse urban setting. Through fiction, Zephaniah contributes to a broader societal conversation about the complexities of multiculturalism and belonging.

- **"Refugee Boy" (2001):**

Another powerful work of fiction, "Refugee Boy," tells the story of a young Ethiopian refugee seeking asylum in the UK. By humanizing the plight of refugees, Zephaniah raises awareness about the harsh realities they face, contributing to discussions on empathy and compassion.

- **"We Are Britain!" (2002):**

In this children's book, Zephaniah celebrates diversity and multiculturalism, instilling important values in young readers. By promoting inclusivity, the book has a positive societal influence, encouraging tolerance and understanding from an early age.

- **"Gangsta Rap" (2004):**

Zephaniah's novel explores themes of youth, crime, and societal expectations. Through the lens of the protagonist's journey, the book prompts reflection on systemic issues and the impact of societal structures on individual choices.

- **"Terror Kid" (2014):**

Addressing contemporary issues, this novel explores the radicalization of a young Muslim boy. Zephaniah's portrayal delves into the complexities surrounding extremism, contributing to discussions on social factors influencing radicalization.

- **Autobiography - "The Life and Rhymes of Benjamin Zephaniah" (2018):**

By sharing his life story, Zephaniah provides insights into his own experiences with racism, activism, and personal growth. This autobiographical work contributes to broader discussions on identity, resilience, and the pursuit of social change.

Through these impactful literary works, Benjamin Zephaniah not only showcases his literary prowess but also engages with pressing societal issues. His writings serve as catalysts for reflection, empathy, and dialogue, fostering a positive influence on readers and contributing to a more nuanced understanding of the world.

Chapter Four: Activism and Advocacy

Benjamin Zephaniah's activism and advocacy are integral components of his influential legacy. Here are key aspects of his commitment to social and political causes:

- **Anti-Racism Advocacy:**

Zephaniah has been a steadfast advocate against racism, using his platform to speak out against discriminatory practices and racial injustice. Through his poetry, writings, and public engagements, he addresses the systemic challenges faced by marginalized communities.

- **Human Rights Advocacy:**

Zephaniah is known for his dedication to human rights causes. His work extends to issues such as freedom of expression, justice, and equality. By actively engaging with human rights organizations, he contributes to ongoing efforts to protect and promote fundamental rights.

- ### Protest and Grassroots Movements:

Zephaniah has been actively involved in grassroots movements and protests. His presence and voice at demonstrations amplify the collective call for social change. Whether participating in anti-apartheid protests or addressing contemporary issues, he stands as a visible advocate for societal transformation.

- ### Environmental Activism:

Zephaniah has expressed concerns about environmental issues and climate change. His advocacy includes raising awareness about the impact of human activities on the planet, reflecting a broader commitment to the well-being of both people and the environment.

- **Anti-Imperialism Stance:**

Zephaniah has taken a critical stance against imperialism and its global implications. His writings and speeches reflect a commitment to dismantling structures of power that perpetuate inequality on a global scale.

- **Engagement with Educational Initiatives:**

Zephaniah has contributed to educational initiatives focused on promoting inclusivity, tolerance, and understanding. Through his works, particularly those targeted at younger audiences, he actively participates in shaping a more inclusive and informed generation.

- **Public Speaking and Lectures:**

Zephaniah's advocacy extends to public speaking engagements and lectures, where he shares insights on social issues, literature, and activism. His ability to connect with diverse audiences enhances the impact of his advocacy efforts.

Benjamin Zephaniah's activism is characterized by a bold and unyielding commitment to challenging societal norms, addressing injustice, and advocating for positive change. Through his multifaceted approach, he continues to inspire others to engage in critical conversations and contribute to a more just and equitable world.

Zephaniah's commitment to social and political causes

Benjamin Zephaniah's commitment to social and political causes is deeply rooted in his personal experiences and a profound belief in using his influence for positive change. Here are key aspects of his commitment:

- **Championing Racial Equality:**

Zephaniah is a vocal advocate against racism, consistently addressing the challenges faced by marginalized communities. His poetry and writings tackle racial injustice, challenging societal norms and fostering dialogue about the need for equality.

- **Human Rights Defender:**

Zephaniah's commitment extends to the broader spectrum of human rights. He actively engages with issues related to freedom of expression, justice, and the fundamental rights of individuals. His advocacy aligns with the principles of human dignity and fairness.

- **Anti-Apartheid Activism:**

Zephaniah has a history of involvement in anti-apartheid activism. His support for the movement against racial segregation in South Africa reflects a lifelong dedication to combating institutionalized oppression.

- **Environmental Activism:**

Beyond social issues, Zephaniah is engaged in environmental activism. Concerned about the impact of human activities on the planet, he advocates for sustainable practices and increased awareness of environmental challenges.

- ## Critique of Imperialism:

Zephaniah takes a critical stance against imperialism, highlighting its impact on global inequality. His writings and public statements reflect a commitment to dismantling structures of power that perpetuate disparities on an international scale.

- ## Advocacy for Peace:

Zephaniah promotes a message of peace and understanding, actively opposing violence and conflict. Through his art and public engagements, he encourages dialogue and cooperation as essential components of a harmonious society.

- ## Educational Initiatives:

Zephaniah actively contributes to educational initiatives aimed at fostering inclusivity and tolerance. His commitment to shaping the minds of future generations underscores his belief in the transformative power of education.

- **Participation in Grassroots Movements:**

Zephaniah is known for his involvement in grassroots movements and protests. By actively participating in demonstrations, he amplifies the collective call for social justice and societal transformation.

Overall, Benjamin Zephaniah's commitment to social and political causes is characterized by a consistent and fearless dedication to addressing injustices, challenging oppressive systems, and advocating for a more equitable and compassionate world. His influence extends beyond his artistic contributions, embodying the role of a socially engaged and impactful public figure.

Involvement in activism, including anti-racism and human rights

Benjamin Zephaniah's involvement in activism, particularly in the realms of anti-racism and human rights, underscores his commitment to societal change. Here are key aspects of his activism in these areas:

- **Anti-Racism Advocacy:**

Zephaniah has been a tireless advocate against racism, using his platform to address systemic racial inequalities. Through his poetry, writings, and public engagements, he challenges discriminatory practices and advocates for a more inclusive and equitable society.

- **Campaigns Against Apartheid:**

Zephaniah has a history of active participation in campaigns against apartheid, particularly focusing on the anti-apartheid movement in South Africa.

His efforts contributed to raising awareness about the oppressive regime and garnering support for global actions against apartheid.

- **Promoting Racial Harmony:**

Beyond direct activism, Zephaniah promotes racial harmony and understanding through his work. His writings often explore themes of cultural diversity, tolerance, and unity, fostering dialogue on the importance of embracing differences.

- **Human Rights Defenders:**

Zephaniah aligns himself with the broader human rights movement. He advocates for the protection of basic human rights, emphasizing principles such as freedom of expression, justice, and equality.

- ## Challenging Institutionalized Discrimination:

Through his art and public statements, Zephaniah confronts institutionalized discrimination. His activism addresses not only individual acts of racism but also the need for systemic changes to eradicate deeply rooted inequalities.

- ## Global Perspectives:

Zephaniah's activism extends to a global scale, where he addresses human rights abuses and injustices beyond national borders. His international perspective contributes to a broader understanding of interconnected struggles for justice.

- ## Educational Initiatives:

Zephaniah actively engages in educational initiatives to combat racism and promote human rights awareness. By participating in discussions, lectures, and workshops, he contributes to shaping informed perspectives on these crucial issues.

- **Participation in Protests:**

Zephaniah has participated in various protests and demonstrations to express his opposition to discriminatory policies and social injustice. His physical presence at these events amplifies the collective voice against racism and human rights violations.

Benjamin Zephaniah's activism serves as a testament to his belief in the power of art and advocacy to bring about positive social change. His multifaceted approach contributes to ongoing conversations about anti-racism, human rights, and the imperative for a more just and inclusive world.

Reflection on his role as a public figure and advocate

Benjamin Zephaniah's role as a public figure and advocate is characterized by a profound dedication to using his influence for positive societal change. Here are reflections on his impactful role:

- **Amplifying Marginalized Voices:**

Zephaniah serves as a vocal advocate for marginalized communities, utilizing his platform to amplify their voices. His commitment to addressing issues of racism, inequality, and injustice reflects a deep sense of responsibility to create space for those often unheard.

- **Fusing Art with Advocacy:**

The seamless integration of art and advocacy distinguishes Zephaniah's role. His poetry, writings, and music serve as powerful mediums for conveying messages of social change. By fusing creativity with activism, he expands the reach of his advocacy to diverse audiences.

- **Challenging Norms Through Art:**

Zephaniah challenges societal norms and confronts uncomfortable truths through his artistic expressions. His role as a provocateur in the cultural landscape prompts critical reflections on issues such as racism, imperialism, and human rights.

- **Global Citizenship:**

His international perspective positions him as a global citizen and advocate. By addressing issues on a global scale, Zephaniah contributes to a broader understanding of interconnected struggles and emphasizes the shared responsibility for creating a just world.

- ## **Educational Impact:**

Zephaniah's engagement in educational initiatives demonstrates a commitment to shaping the minds of future generations. By participating in discussions, lectures, and workshops, he influences perceptions and encourages critical thinking on matters of social justice.

- ## **Participation in Grassroots Movements:**

Actively participating in grassroots movements and protests, Zephaniah embodies a hands-on approach to advocacy. His physical presence at demonstrations underscores his solidarity with the causes he champions, connecting him with the grassroots level of societal change.

- **Lifelong Commitment:**

Zephaniah's activism spans decades, illustrating a lifelong commitment to causes he holds dear. His enduring dedication to anti-racism, human rights, and environmental issues underscores a sustained effort to contribute to lasting societal transformation.

- **Cultural Influence:**

As a public figure, Zephaniah's cultural influence extends beyond traditional boundaries. His impact on literature, poetry, and music positions him as a cultural icon whose advocacy goes hand in hand with his artistic legacy.

In essence, Benjamin Zephaniah's role as a public figure and advocate is one of profound significance. His ability to bridge the worlds of art and activism exemplifies a holistic approach to creating positive

Benjamin Zephaniah

change, inspiring others to engage with critical societal issues and contribute to building a more just and equitable world.

Chapter Five: Personal Life

Benjamin Zephaniah's personal life, while often private, provides glimpses into the man behind the public persona. Here are key aspects:

- **Family Background:**

Zephaniah was born on April 15, 1958, in Birmingham, UK, to Jamaican parents. His cultural heritage and upbringing in Handsworth, Birmingham, significantly influenced his identity and artistic expressions.

- **Early Experiences:**

Growing up in a multicultural environment, Zephaniah's early experiences exposed him to the challenges of racial tension and social change. These experiences would later become central themes in his poetry and activism.

- ## Education:

Despite facing challenges and dropping out of school at a young age, Zephaniah is largely autodidactic. His love for literature and self-directed learning contributed to his development as a poet and writer.

- ## Artistic Influences:

Zephaniah's love for the arts, including reggae music and poetry, began to shape his artistic sensibilities from an early age. The cultural vibrancy of Birmingham, combined with global influences, played a role in his eclectic artistic expressions.

- ## Romantic Relationships:

He was in matrimony with Amina, a theater administrator, for a duration of twelve years. In 2001, the couple underwent a divorce.

- ## Public and Private Life:

As a public figure, Zephaniah has navigated the challenge of balancing his public and private life. While openly sharing aspects of his activism and creative pursuits, he maintains a level of privacy regarding personal details.

- ## Philosophy and Beliefs:

Zephaniah's personal philosophy aligns with his advocacy for social justice, equality, and human rights. His writings and public statements reflect a commitment to challenging societal norms and fostering positive change.

- ## Vegan Lifestyle:

Zephaniah is known for his vegan lifestyle, advocating for animal rights and environmental sustainability. His commitment to ethical choices extends to his broader philosophy on living in harmony with the planet.

While specific details about Benjamin Zephaniah's personal life remain private, his journey from a challenging upbringing to a celebrated artist and activist showcases resilience, self-discovery, and a commitment to making a positive impact on the world.

Insights into Zephaniah's personal relationships and family

Benjamin Zephaniah tends to keep details of his personal relationships and family life private, and specific insights into these aspects of his life may not be readily available in the public domain. Zephaniah is known for focusing on broader social and political themes in his public work, and he has maintained a level of privacy regarding the more intimate aspects of his personal life.

His family background, as mentioned earlier, includes being born to Jamaican parents in Birmingham. While his poetry and writings occasionally touch upon personal emotions and experiences, the specific details of his personal relationships, such as romantic partnerships or family dynamics, are not extensively disclosed in the public sphere.

Zephaniah's emphasis on issues related to race, social justice, and equality has been a central theme in his artistic and activist endeavors. These aspects of his work often take precedence in public discussions about him. As with many public figures, the choice to keep certain aspects of personal life private allows Zephaniah to maintain a boundary between his public persona and personal relationships.

Balancing public life with private experiences

Balancing public life with private experiences is a delicate task, and Benjamin Zephaniah has navigated this balance with a nuanced approach. Here are some insights into how he manages this:

- **Artistic Expression:**

Zephaniah often uses his art, particularly poetry and writings, as a means of expressing personal experiences. While the themes may touch upon intimate aspects of life, he maintains a level of abstraction that allows for interpretation without divulging specific details.

- **Focus on Social Issues:**

Zephaniah's public presence is primarily defined by his activism and engagement with social issues. By focusing on broader societal themes, he directs public attention toward the causes he is passionate about, while keeping more personal aspects of his life relatively private.

• Selective Disclosure:

While he shares insights into his upbringing, cultural influences, and broader philosophies, Zephaniah is selective about disclosing specific details of his personal life. This intentional choice allows him to control the narrative surrounding his public persona.

• Maintaining Privacy:

Zephaniah understands the importance of maintaining a degree of privacy. By keeping certain aspects of his personal life away from the public spotlight, he can preserve a sense of intimacy and protect those closest to him.

- **Ethical Lifestyle Choices:**

Zephaniah's public engagement often extends to ethical lifestyle choices, such as his veganism. These choices reflect personal values but are presented in a way that aligns with his broader advocacy for social and environmental issues.

- **Artistic Persona vs. Personal Self:**

Zephaniah's public persona is shaped by his artistic expressions and advocacy work. While these may draw inspiration from personal experiences, there is a distinction between the persona presented in his creative works and his private self.

Balancing public and private life requires a strategic and intentional approach, especially for individuals in the public eye. Zephaniah's ability to share meaningful insights into his experiences while maintaining a level of privacy contributes to the complexity and authenticity of his public persona.

Chapter Six: Challenges and Triumphs

Challenges:

- **Early Struggles:**

Benjamin Zephaniah faced significant challenges in his early life, including dropping out of school at a young age. These early struggles shaped his resilience and determination to overcome obstacles.

- **Encountering Racism:**

Growing up in a multicultural environment, Zephaniah experienced firsthand the challenges of racial tension. Racism and systemic inequalities became recurring themes in his work as he sought to address and combat these issues.

- **Activism Amidst Opposition:**

Zephaniah's commitment to activism, particularly in anti-racism and human rights, exposed him to opposition and criticism. Addressing controversial topics often comes with challenges, yet he persevered in using his platform to advocate for positive change.

- **Navigating Public Scrutiny:**

Being a public figure, Zephaniah has had to navigate the scrutiny that comes with fame. Balancing a public persona with personal privacy requires thoughtful consideration and can be challenging in the age of media attention.

Triumphs:
- **Artistic Success:**

Zephaniah's breakthrough in the UK poetry scene marked a triumph in the realm of performance poetry. His ability to captivate audiences and redefine the possibilities of poetic expression contributed to his lasting impact on the literary landscape.

- **International Recognition:**

Achieving recognition on an international scale, Zephaniah's influence extends beyond national borders. His work has resonated with audiences globally, solidifying him as a prominent figure in literature and activism.

- **Literary Legacy:**

The publication of numerous poetry collections, novels, and children's books has left an enduring literary legacy. Zephaniah's works continue to be studied, celebrated, and appreciated for their social commentary, creativity, and linguistic innovation.

- **Honors and Awards:**

Benjamin Zephaniah has received honors and awards for his contributions to literature and activism, including being appointed as a Commander of the Order of the British Empire (CBE) in 2008. These accolades recognize the impact of his work on a national level.

- **Advocacy Impact:**

Zephaniah's advocacy efforts have contributed to raising awareness about issues such as racism, human rights, and environmental concerns. His ability to use his platform for positive change showcases the triumph of influence and impact in the realms of social justice.

In navigating challenges and celebrating triumphs, Benjamin Zephaniah's journey reflects a narrative of resilience, artistic achievement, and a commitment to fostering positive societal change.

Overview of obstacles faced throughout his journey

Obstacles Faced by Benjamin Zephaniah Throughout His Journey:

- **Educational Challenges:**

Zephaniah faced early educational challenges, dropping out of school at a young age. Overcoming this hurdle required a commitment to self-directed learning and a passion for literature that would later define his artistic path.

- **Racial Tension:**

Growing up in Birmingham during a period of racial tension, Zephaniah encountered firsthand the challenges of racism and discrimination. These experiences became significant influences on his poetry and activism.

- ### **Systemic Inequality:**

Zephaniah's commitment to addressing systemic inequalities, especially those related to race, led him to confront deeply rooted societal issues. This advocacy, while vital, presented obstacles in the form of resistance, opposition, and the need for sustained efforts.

- ### **Navigating the Literary Scene:**

Breaking into the literary scene, particularly with a unique form of performance poetry, posed challenges. Zephaniah's unconventional approach faced initial skepticism, but his persistence and innovative style ultimately triumphed.

- ### **Public Scrutiny:**

As a public figure, Zephaniah has had to navigate public scrutiny and the challenges that come with fame. Balancing personal privacy with the demands of a public persona requires careful consideration and resilience.

- **Controversial Topics:**

Addressing controversial topics in his poetry and activism, including anti-racism and human rights, exposed Zephaniah to opposition and criticism. Tackling such sensitive issues comes with its own set of challenges, but he remained steadfast in his commitment to social justice.

- **Media Attention:**

Dealing with media attention, especially in an era of increasing visibility, requires a strategic approach. Zephaniah's journey involves managing the impacts of media coverage on both his personal and professional life.

- **Global Advocacy:**

Extending his activism to global issues, Zephaniah faced the challenge of addressing diverse and interconnected challenges on an international scale. Tackling issues like imperialism and global inequality requires a nuanced understanding and a persistent commitment.

Despite these obstacles, Benjamin Zephaniah's journey reflects a story of resilience, creativity, and a determination to use his voice to advocate for positive change. Each challenge became an opportunity for growth and a catalyst for the impactful trajectory of his life and career.

How Zephaniah navigated challenges and achieved success

Benjamin Zephaniah's Navigation of Challenges and Achievements:

- **Resilience and Self-Directed Learning:**

Faced with educational challenges, Zephaniah demonstrated resilience by pursuing self-directed learning. His passion for literature and poetry became the foundation for his artistic journey.

- **Transforming Personal Experiences into Art:**

Zephaniah channeled the racial tensions he experienced in Birmingham into his poetry, transforming personal challenges into powerful artistic expressions. His ability to turn adversity into creative fuel marked a turning point in his artistic identity.

- **Innovative Approach to Poetry:**

Overcoming skepticism in the literary scene, Zephaniah's innovative approach to performance poetry challenged traditional norms. His dynamic and rhythmic style captured audiences, establishing him as a trailblazer in the realm of spoken word.

- **Staying True to Controversial Themes:**

Zephaniah remained committed to addressing controversial themes, such as anti-racism and human rights, despite facing opposition. His unwavering dedication to speaking out against injustice contributed to the societal impact of his work.

• **Balancing Public and Private Life:**

Navigating public scrutiny and media attention, Zephaniah found a balance between his public persona and personal privacy. This strategic approach allowed him to maintain authenticity while managing the challenges of being in the public eye.

• **International Impact:**

Zephaniah successfully expanded his activism to global issues, demonstrating a nuanced understanding of interconnected challenges. His ability to address international concerns contributed to his recognition as a globally influential figure.

- **Diversification of Artistic Endeavors:**

Beyond poetry, Zephaniah diversified his artistic pursuits into music, novels, children's literature, and playwriting. This versatility not only showcased his breadth of talent but also expanded his reach and influence.

- **Advocacy Through Honors and Awards:**

Recognition through honors and awards, such as being appointed a Commander of the Order of the British Empire (CBE), elevated Zephaniah's advocacy on a national level. These accolades acknowledged not only his artistic contributions but also his impact on societal issues.

- **Engaging with Education:**

Zephaniah actively engaged with education, contributing to the shaping of future generations. His involvement in educational initiatives demonstrated a commitment to fostering understanding and inclusivity.

Benjamin Zephaniah's journey is marked by a combination of artistic innovation, resilience in the face of challenges, and a steadfast commitment to using his platform for positive change. His ability to navigate obstacles while staying true to his principles has contributed to a lasting and impactful career.

Reflection on the impact of his work on overcoming adversity

Benjamin Zephaniah's work has had a profound impact on overcoming adversity, serving as both a source of inspiration and a catalyst for societal change. Here's a reflection on the transformative influence of his contributions:

- **Empowering Marginalized Voices:**

Zephaniah's poetry amplifies the voices of those who often go unheard, especially individuals facing racial injustice and systemic inequalities. By expressing the challenges of adversity through his art, he empowers marginalized communities to reclaim their narratives.

- **Redefining Perceptions Through Poetry:**

Through his innovative approach to performance poetry, Zephaniah has redefined perceptions of what poetry can be. His dynamic and rhythmic style broke down barriers, showcasing that art can be a powerful tool for self-expression and overcoming societal norms.

- **Advocacy Through Creativity:**

Zephaniah's commitment to addressing controversial themes in his work, such as anti-racism and human rights, contributes to dismantling systemic adversity. His poems serve as a call to action, inspiring individuals to engage in conversations and activism that challenge oppressive structures.

- **Personal Transformation:**

Zephaniah's personal journey from early struggles to international acclaim exemplifies how creativity and resilience can lead to personal transformation. By channeling his experiences into art, he not only transcended adversity but also transformed it into a force for positive change.

- **Educational Impact:**

Zephaniah's engagement with education reflects a commitment to breaking down barriers for future generations. By participating in educational initiatives, he provides pathways for young individuals to overcome challenges and pursue knowledge as a means of empowerment.

- ## Cultural Impact:

Zephaniah's influence extends beyond literature to impact culture and societal perspectives. His works challenge ingrained prejudices and stereotypes, fostering a cultural shift towards inclusivity and understanding.

- ## Global Dialogue:

Through addressing international issues in his activism and art, Zephaniah encourages a global dialogue on overcoming shared adversities. His work inspires cross-cultural conversations, fostering a sense of interconnectedness in the face of global challenges.

- ## Legacy of Empathy and Compassion:

Zephaniah's body of work leaves a lasting legacy of empathy and compassion. By depicting the struggles of individuals facing adversity, he fosters understanding and prompts collective action towards a more just and compassionate society.

In essence, Benjamin Zephaniah's impact on overcoming adversity lies in his ability to transform personal and societal challenges into a call for resilience, justice, and positive change. His work serves as a testament to the transformative power of art and activism in navigating and ultimately overcoming adversity.

Chapter Seven: Legacy

Legacy of Benjamin Zephaniah:

- **Literary Innovation:**

Zephaniah's innovative approach to performance poetry and spoken word has left an indelible mark on the literary landscape. His rhythmic and dynamic style challenged traditional norms, inspiring a new generation of poets and performers.

- **Social Justice Advocacy:**

The legacy of Zephaniah is deeply rooted in his unwavering commitment to social justice. His activism against racism, human rights abuses, and systemic inequalities continues to inspire individuals and movements globally.

- **Empowering   Marginalized Communities:**

Through his poetry, Zephaniah empowers marginalized communities by providing a platform for their voices. His work fosters a sense of agency and identity, encouraging individuals to speak out against injustice.

- **Global Impact:**

Zephaniah's influence extends beyond national borders, contributing to a global dialogue on issues of justice and equality. His activism and art resonate with audiences around the world, connecting people through shared struggles and aspirations.

- **Educational Contribution:**

Zephaniah's engagement with education, both through his own journey and involvement in educational initiatives, forms part of his legacy. He leaves a lasting impact on shaping the minds of future generations, emphasizing the transformative power of learning.

- **Cultural Shift:**

Zephaniah's contributions have played a role in shaping cultural perceptions. His writings challenge stereotypes and prejudices, fostering a cultural shift towards greater inclusivity, understanding, and appreciation of diversity.

- **Versatility in Artistic Expression:**

The legacy of Zephaniah extends beyond poetry to encompass music, novels, children's literature, and plays. His versatility showcases the interconnectedness of various artistic forms in addressing social issues.

- ## Inspiration for Activism:

Zephaniah's life and work serve as an inspiration for activists and advocates. His courage to address controversial topics and his dedication to effecting positive change inspire others to use their platforms for social impact.

- ## Pioneer of Spoken Word:

As a pioneer of the spoken word genre, Zephaniah's legacy includes redefining the possibilities of poetry. He has opened doors for poets and artists to explore new avenues of creative expression, emphasizing the spoken word's potential for societal commentary.

- ## Cultural Icon:

Benjamin Zephaniah's influence as a cultural icon is reflected in his enduring impact on literature, music, and activism.

His legacy continues to shape conversations around race, equality, and the power of art in effecting change.

In sum, Benjamin Zephaniah's legacy is multifaceted, encompassing literary innovation, social justice advocacy, cultural influence, and an enduring commitment to empowering communities. His impact on both the arts and societal consciousness positions him as a figure whose legacy resonates across generations and geographical boundaries.

Examination of Benjamin Zephaniah's lasting influence

Examination of Benjamin Zephaniah's Lasting Influence:

- **Literary Innovation:**

Zephaniah's influence on literature is marked by his innovative approach to performance poetry. He redefined the boundaries of poetic expression, showcasing the potential of spoken word as a dynamic and accessible medium for social commentary.

- **Activism as Art:**

His lasting influence lies in the seamless integration of activism and art. Zephaniah's ability to use poetry as a tool for advocacy set a precedent for artists globally, illustrating the transformative power of creative expression in addressing societal issues.

- ## **Amplifying Marginalized Voices:**

Zephaniah's legacy includes his dedication to amplifying the voices of marginalized communities. By centering his work on themes of justice and equality, he paved the way for a more inclusive representation within the literary and artistic landscape.

- ## **Global Recognition:**

Zephaniah's impact extends internationally, contributing to a global dialogue on social justice. His work resonates with diverse audiences, transcending cultural and geographical boundaries and fostering a sense of shared humanity.

- ## **Educational Empowerment:**

His influence on education is evident in his engagement with learning initiatives. Zephaniah's commitment to education as a means of empowerment has inspired educators and students alike, emphasizing the transformative potential of knowledge.

- **Cultural Resonance:**

Zephaniah's influence on culture is characterized by his efforts to challenge stereotypes and reshape cultural perceptions. His work prompts critical conversations about race, identity, and societal norms, contributing to a broader cultural shift.

- **Legacy in Spoken Word:**

As a pioneer in spoken word, Zephaniah's influence endures in the continued popularity and evolution of this genre. His contributions have inspired a new generation of poets and performers to use their voices for social change.

- **Cross-Genre Impact:**

Zephaniah's versatility across genres, including music and literature, showcases his enduring influence. His ability to navigate various artistic forms while maintaining a consistent commitment to social justice sets a precedent for artists exploring interdisciplinary expressions.

- **Inspiration for Future Activists:**

Zephaniah's legacy serves as an inspiration for future activists and advocates. His fearless approach to addressing controversial topics and using his platform for positive change encourages others to engage in impactful activism through their chosen mediums.

- **Iconic Cultural Figure:**

Benjamin Zephaniah's lasting influence positions him as an iconic cultural figure.

His impact on literature, spoken word, and activism continues to shape discussions on race, justice, and the role of art in societal transformation.

In conclusion, Benjamin Zephaniah's lasting influence is characterized by his profound contributions to literature, activism, and culture. His ability to transcend artistic boundaries, amplify marginalized voices, and inspire social change cements his legacy as a transformative figure in the realms of creativity and advocacy.

Evaluation of his contribution to literature, activism, and culture

Evaluation of Benjamin Zephaniah's Contribution:

- **Literature:**

Innovation in Poetry: Zephaniah's contribution to literature is marked by his innovative approach to poetry. His dynamic and rhythmic style in performance poetry challenged traditional norms, expanding the possibilities of poetic expression.

Diverse Literary Output: With numerous poetry collections, novels, children's books, and plays, Zephaniah showcased versatility in literary forms, leaving a diverse and impactful body of work.

- **Activism:**

Championing Social Justice: Zephaniah's activism against racism, human rights abuses, and systemic inequalities has been a cornerstone of his contribution. Through his art and public engagements, he consistently advocates for positive societal change.

Global Impact: His activism extends globally, addressing international issues and contributing to a broader conversation on interconnected social challenges. Zephaniah's commitment to global justice showcases the breadth of his advocacy.

- **Culture:**

Reshaping Cultural Perceptions: Zephaniah's cultural impact is evident in his efforts to challenge stereotypes and reshape cultural perceptions. His work prompts critical conversations about race, identity, and societal norms, fostering a cultural shift.

Versatility Across Genres: Contributing to both literature and music, Zephaniah's versatility showcases his influence on multiple cultural fronts. His ability to navigate various artistic forms has left a lasting imprint on cultural expressions.

- **Education:**

Empowering Through Education: Zephaniah's engagement with education reflects a commitment to empowering individuals through knowledge. His involvement in educational initiatives underscores the transformative potential of learning in overcoming societal challenges.

- **Legacy:**

Lasting Impact: Benjamin Zephaniah's legacy is enduring, with his influence seen in the continued popularity of spoken word, the exploration of diverse literary forms, and the ongoing conversations around social justice and cultural representation.

Inspiration for Future Generations: His legacy serves as an inspiration for future generations of artists, activists, and educators. Zephaniah's fearless approach and dedication to positive change provide a blueprint for those seeking to use their talents for societal impact.

In summary, Benjamin Zephaniah's contribution to literature, activism, and culture is multifaceted and impactful. His innovative literary expressions, unwavering advocacy for social justice, cultural resonance, educational engagement, and lasting legacy collectively position him as a transformative figure whose influence spans artistic, societal, and educational realms.

Consideration of his ongoing impact and relevance

Ongoing Impact and Relevance of Benjamin Zephaniah:

- **Literary Influence:**

Continued Recognition: Zephaniah's impact on literature endures as his works continue to be studied and celebrated. His influence on contemporary poets and writers is reflected in the ongoing exploration of innovative and dynamic literary forms.

- **Activism and Social Justice:**

Relevance in Current Movements: Zephaniah's activism remains relevant in the context of current social justice movements. His unwavering commitment to addressing racism, inequality, and human rights abuses resonates with ongoing struggles for justice around the world.

- ## Cultural Relevance:

Addressing Contemporary Issues: Zephaniah's work, addressing themes of race, identity, and societal norms, remains culturally relevant. The continued relevance of these themes ensures that his contributions remain integral to contemporary cultural conversations.

- ## Educational Impact:

Inspiring Educational Initiatives: Zephaniah's engagement with education inspires ongoing initiatives that use learning as a tool for empowerment. His legacy encourages educators to foster critical thinking and inclusivity in educational settings.

- ## Legacy in Spoken Word:

Influence on Contemporary Artists: Zephaniah's influence on spoken word endures, with contemporary artists drawing inspiration from his dynamic and rhythmic style. The continued popularity of spoken word as a medium reflects the lasting impact of his contributions.

- **Global Perspectives:**

Addressing Global Challenges: Zephaniah's global perspective in activism remains relevant as contemporary issues increasingly span international borders. His commitment to addressing global challenges provides a framework for understanding interconnected struggles.

- **Inspiration for Future Generations:**

Impact on Emerging Artists: Zephaniah's ongoing impact is evident in the work of emerging artists who find inspiration in his fearlessness, versatility, and dedication to positive change. His legacy serves as a guiding influence for those navigating the intersection of art and activism.

• Digital Age Relevance:

Accessible Platforms: In the digital age, Zephaniah's work remains accessible to a wide audience through online platforms. His continued presence in digital spaces ensures that new generations can engage with his art and ideas.

• Environmental Advocacy:

Relevance in Environmental Discourse: Zephaniah's advocacy for the environment aligns with contemporary concerns about climate change and sustainability. His voice in environmental issues remains pertinent as global awareness of ecological challenges grows.

• Cultural Icon Status:

Enduring Cultural Icon: Benjamin Zephaniah's status as a cultural icon persists. His ongoing impact is seen in how his contributions continue to shape discussions on race, equality, and the transformative power of art within contemporary cultural landscapes.

In conclusion, Benjamin Zephaniah's ongoing impact and relevance are evident across literary, activist, cultural, and educational domains. His ability to address current issues, inspire new generations, and remain a cultural touchstone underscores the enduring significance of his contributions.

Benjamin Zephaniah

His death

At the age of 65, Zephaniah passed away on December 7, 2023, following an eight-week diagnosis of a brain tumor.

Chapter Eight: Conclusion

In conclusion, Benjamin Zephaniah emerges as a transformative figure whose influence extends across the realms of literature, activism, and culture. His innovative approach to performance poetry challenged traditional norms, paving the way for a new era of creative expression. Zephaniah's unwavering commitment to social justice, particularly in addressing racism and human rights abuses, positions him as a stalwart advocate whose impact transcends national borders.

His cultural resonance is evident in the ongoing conversations about race, identity, and societal norms, reflecting the enduring relevance of his work. Zephaniah's educational engagement emphasizes the transformative power of learning, inspiring future generations to use knowledge as a tool for empowerment and change.

As a literary icon, Zephaniah's influence persists in the continued exploration of diverse literary forms, with his legacy shaping the trajectory of contemporary poets and writers. His legacy in spoken word endures, and his multifaceted contributions to music, literature, and activism showcase the interconnectedness of these art forms in addressing societal challenges.

Benjamin Zephaniah's ongoing impact is characterized by his ability to remain relevant in the face of evolving social, cultural, and global landscapes. His legacy serves as an enduring source of inspiration for artists, activists, educators, and individuals seeking to use their voices for positive societal transformation. As a cultural icon, Zephaniah's contributions continue to reverberate, reminding us of the transformative power that art and activism can wield in shaping a more just and equitable world.

Summarizing the key aspects of Benjamin Zephaniah's life

Summary of Key Aspects of Benjamin Zephaniah's Life:

- **Early Life and Upbringing:**

Born on April 15, 1958, in Birmingham, UK, to Jamaican parents.
Raised in the multicultural environment of Handsworth, Birmingham, shaping his cultural identity.

- **Educational Challenges and Autodidactic Pursuits:**

Faced educational challenges, dropping out of school at a young age.
Embarked on self-directed learning, driven by a passion for literature and poetry.

- **Cultural Influences and Racial Tensions:**

Growing up during a period of racial tension in Birmingham.
Early experiences with racism and systemic inequalities influenced his worldview and artistic expressions.

- **Entry into Literature and Poetry:**

Influences from reggae music and diverse artistic forms.
Early encounters with poetry and activism that laid the foundation for his artistic journey.

- **Rise to Prominence in the UK Poetry Scene:**

Breakthrough with innovative performance poetry, challenging traditional norms.

Became a leading figure in the UK poetry scene, captivating audiences with his dynamic style.

- **Diversification of Artistic Pursuits:**

Exploration of various art forms, including music, novels, children's literature, and plays.
Versatility showcased in his ability to navigate different creative mediums.

- **National and International Recognition:**

Achieved recognition on a national and international scale for his contributions to literature and activism.
Appointed as a Commander of the Order of the British Empire (CBE) in 2008.

- **Literary Legacy and Notable Works:**

Published numerous poetry collections, novels, and children's books.
Literary legacy marked by innovative forms, social commentary, and linguistic creativity.

- **Activism and Advocacy:**

Lifelong commitment to addressing social issues, including racism, human rights, and environmental concerns.
Active participation in grassroots movements, protests, and global advocacy.

- **Personal Life:**

Maintained a level of privacy regarding personal relationships and family details.
Known for his vegan lifestyle, advocating for animal rights and environmental sustainability.

- **Balancing Public and Private Life:**

Navigated the challenges of fame while maintaining a distinction between public and private aspects.
Used his platform strategically for societal impact without compromising personal boundaries.

- **Lasting Legacy and Ongoing Impact:**

Legacy characterized by literary innovation, activism, cultural influence, and educational engagement.
Ongoing impact seen in continued recognition, relevance in contemporary movements, and inspiration for future generations.

In essence, Benjamin Zephaniah's life is a tapestry woven with literary brilliance, social activism, and a commitment to positive change. His journey from a challenging upbringing to international acclaim showcases resilience, creativity, and an enduring dedication to making a lasting impact on the world.

Reflecting on the broader significance of his legacy

Benjamin Zephaniah's legacy extends far beyond the realm of individual achievements; it is a testament to the transformative power of art, activism, and unwavering commitment to social justice. The broader significance of his legacy can be observed in several key aspects:

- **Innovative Artistic Expression:**

Zephaniah's legacy underscores the transformative potential of innovative artistic expression. His dynamic and rhythmic performance poetry not only redefined the possibilities of the art form but also inspired a new generation of poets to push creative boundaries.

- ## Intersectionality of Art and Activism:

The significance of his legacy lies in the seamless integration of art and activism. Zephaniah demonstrated that poetry and creative expression can be potent tools for addressing societal issues, challenging systemic injustices, and fostering positive change.

- ## Amplifying Marginalized Voices:

Zephaniah's commitment to amplifying marginalized voices remains a beacon in the broader struggle for inclusivity. His legacy emphasizes the importance of providing a platform for those whose narratives are often overlooked, contributing to a more diverse and representative cultural landscape.

- **Global Relevance of Social Advocacy:**

The global impact of Zephaniah's activism illustrates the broader significance of advocating for social justice on an international scale. His work transcends borders, contributing to a universal dialogue on issues like racism, inequality, and human rights.

- **Educational Empowerment:**

Zephaniah's engagement with education highlights the enduring significance of learning as a tool for empowerment. His legacy encourages a holistic understanding of education as a means not only for personal growth but also for societal transformation.

- ## Cultural Shift and Representation:-

The broader significance of Zephaniah's legacy is evident in its contribution to cultural shifts. By challenging stereotypes and reshaping cultural perceptions, he paved the way for greater inclusivity and a more nuanced understanding of diverse identities within the cultural narrative.

- ## Inspiration for Future Generations:

Perhaps most importantly, Zephaniah's legacy serves as an inspiration for future generations. His fearless approach to addressing controversial topics, versatility across artistic mediums, and dedication to positive change provide a roadmap for individuals seeking to use their talents for societal impact.

• **Enduring Cultural Icon:**

Zephaniah's legacy positions him as an enduring cultural icon whose influence persists across time. His contributions continue to shape contemporary conversations on race, equality, and the intersection of art with activism, emphasizing the enduring power of cultural figures to catalyze change.

In reflection, Benjamin Zephaniah's legacy is a dynamic and multifaceted force, influencing not only the artistic and literary spheres but also resonating deeply in the broader landscape of social change, education, and cultural transformation. His life's work exemplifies the profound impact one individual can have in shaping a more equitable and enlightened world.

Achievements

The BBC Young Playwright's Award went to Zephaniah. In 1998, the University of North London, in 1999, the University of Central England, in 2001, in 2003, at London South Bank University, in 2008, at Exeter University, in 2006, at Westminster University, and in 2008 at Birmingham University, he was granted honorary doctorates. On The Times list of the 50 best postwar writers, he came in at number 48.

Printed in Great Britain
by Amazon

34214420R00069